A Big Job

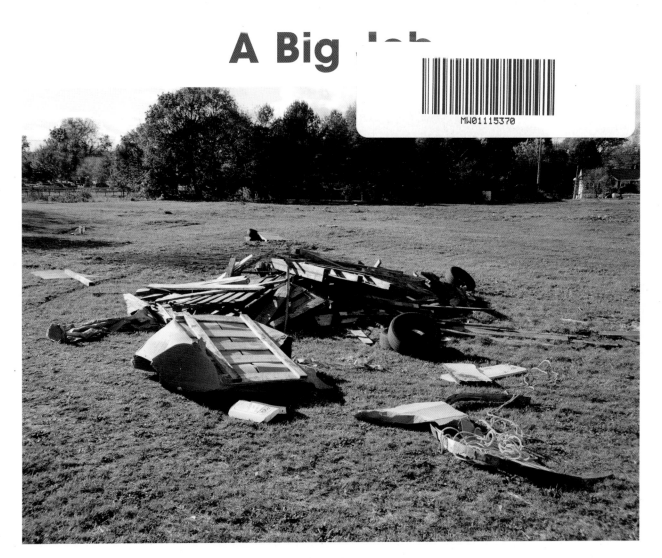

by Gina Russo

The lot is a mess.

Kids can not play.

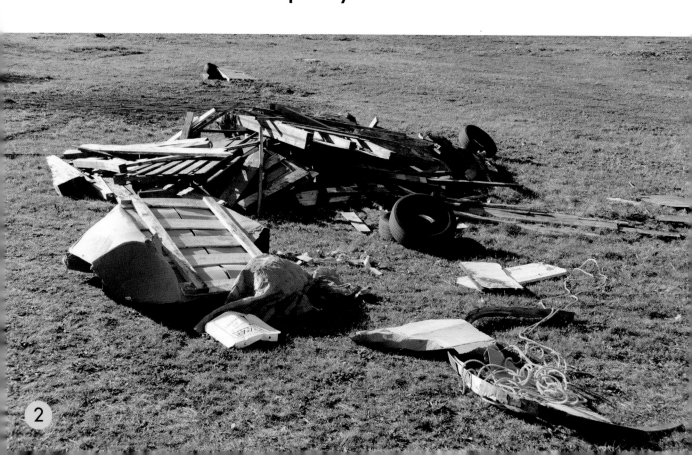

We can fix it.

We have a good plan!

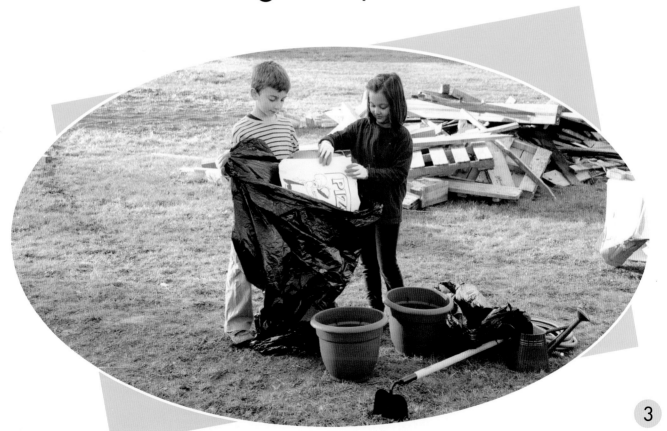

Jill got a hoe.

Jack got a pot.

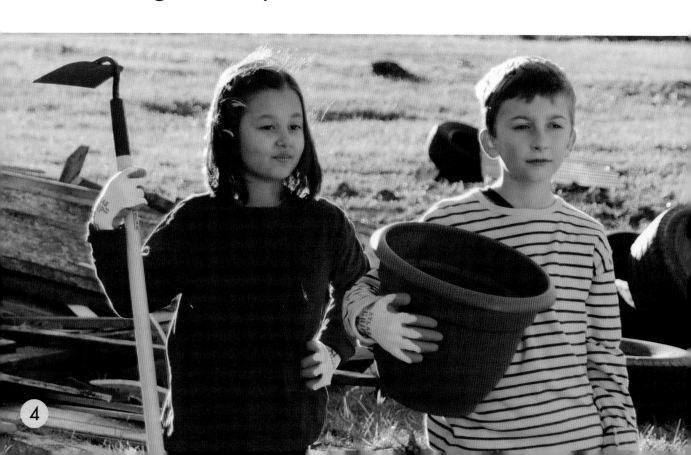

Jill has a can.

Jack has a hose.

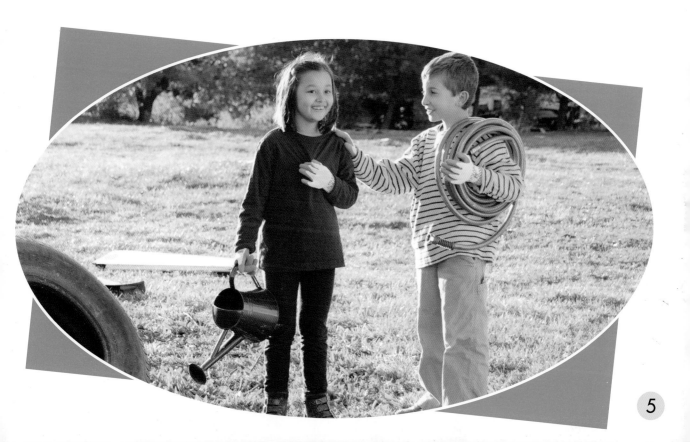

The lot is not a mess!

Kids can jump and hop.

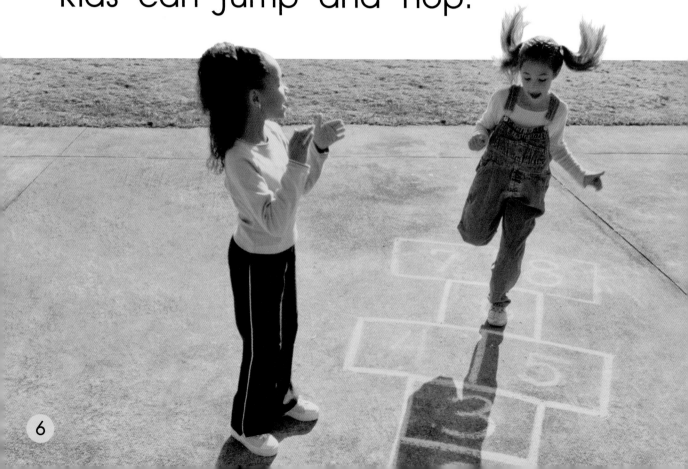

Moms and dads can jog.

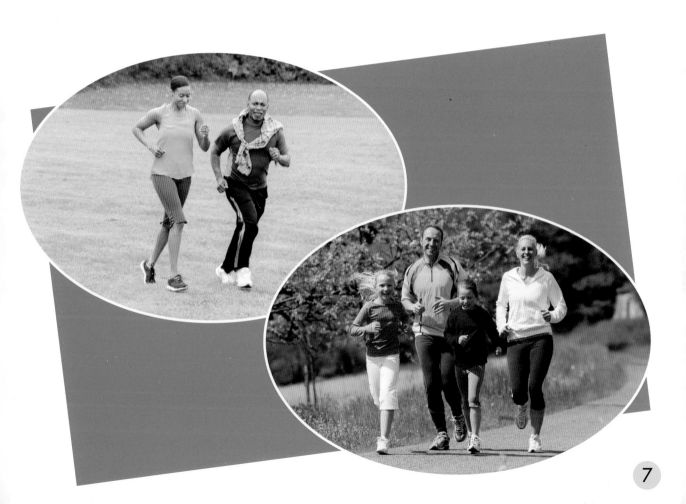

Jill and Jack did a good job!

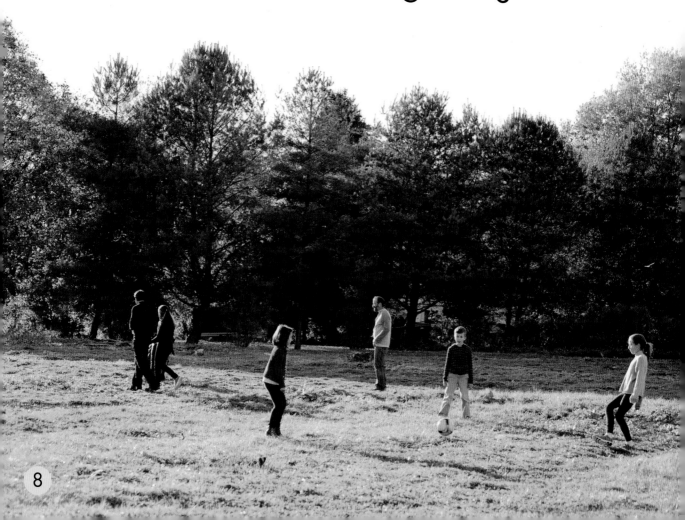